Arthur Baker's Copybook of
of
RENAISSANCE
CALLIGRAPHY

(Mercator's Italic Hand)

With an Introduction by
William Hogarth

DOVER PUBLICATIONS, INC.
NEW YORK

Published in Canada by General Publishing Company, Ltd., 30 Lesmill Road, Don Mills, Toronto, Ontario.
Published in the United Kingdom by Constable and Company, Ltd., 10 Orange Street, London WC2H 7EG.

Arthur Baker's Copybook of Renaissance Calligraphy (Mercator's Italic Hand) is a new work, first published by Dover Publications, Inc., in 1981.

DOVER *Pictorial Archive* SERIES

Arthur Baker's Copybook of Renaissance Calligraphy (Mercator's Italic Hand) belongs to the Dover Pictorial Archive Series. Up to ten letters from it may be used in any single publication or on any single project without payment to or permission from the publisher. Wherever possible include a credit line indicating title, artist and publisher. Please address the publisher for permission to make more extensive use of designs in this volume than that authorized above.
The reproduction of this book in whole is prohibited.

International Standard Book Number: 0-486-24162-9
Library of Congress Catalog Card Number: 81-66494

Manufactured in the United States of America
Dover Publications, Inc.
180 Varick Street
New York, N.Y. 10014

INTRODUCTION

"...those letters called Italic or cursive..."

In 1540, at the age of twenty-eight, Gerardus Mercator issued his writing manual *Literarum Latinarum* at Louvain, site of the famous university, in a part of Flanders that is now in Belgium. The title page referred to the creation of "those letters called Italic or cursive." Calligraphy was but one of Mercator's accomplishments, although he was certainly the peer of the Italian writing masters who were at that time also publishing their manuals: Arrighi, Palatino, Cresci and Tagliente. He admired the humanistic cursive style of writing as most appropriate, with its added swashes, for use in lettering the place names and legends on his maps; for it is his cartography and the famed "Mercator projection" that have made his name known to subsequent generations of nonspecialists, scholars and schoolchildren.

By the time he was twenty-four, Mercator had been educated at Louvain in theology and classical studies, had mastered astronomy, Ptolemaic geography, calligraphy, engraving and the technical skills necessary to become one of the greatest scientific-instrument makers (he later created such instruments for Charles V). As had his Dutch near-contemporary Desiderius Erasmus, Mercator latinized his name (Gerhard Kremer) in the spirit of classical scholarship. His life span (1512–1594) matched almost the whole of the Tudor reign in England; he did, in fact, engrave Camden's map of the British Isles in 1564 (his map of Europe had appeared in 1554). At his death, his ambitious *Atlas of the World* was not quite complete. His unique projection was, and still is, one of the best methods of representing a sphere in segments, or gores, on a flat plane.

With characteristic thoroughness, Arthur Baker has gone back to both the manual and the maps of Mercator, projecting enlargements of the relatively small letterforms in the originals, studying all the details and creating large-scale letters from Mercator's work. The result is rewarding on two levels. First, Mercator's letters are exceptionally fine; unlike his Italian contemporaries, whose instruction pages were cut on wood blocks for printing by specialist craftsmen-engravers, Mercator cut his own printing blocks, thereby retaining the personal "hand" that had inscribed the original pages with a quill.

The second benefit to readers—and viewers, in this image-viewing age—is the latest evidence of the calligraphic brilliance of Arthur Baker, creator of the Dover originals *Calligraphy*, *Calligraphic Alphabets* and *Historic Calligraphic Alphabets*. For here are the finely honed representations stemming from Mercator's originals, as unusual and fresh as we have come to expect from Baker, yet with the necessary disciplined freedom that makes a scribal master's work come alive.

As teacher, creator of hundreds of calligraphic alphabets and typefaces, and as a craftsman applying his skills to inscriptional lettering, book jackets and commercial work, Arthur Baker is the leading figure in what may well be a new renaissance of the craft and art of calligraphy. His total dedication to letters has created disciples for his concept of the "new calligraphy," a rebirth of the gentle humanism that has an almost uncanny affinity with the spirit of Mercator, and with all those whose continuing human concerns have kept alive and available aspirations to knowledge and interpersonal morality.

Current fashionable pessimism would have us believe that, because of the bombardment of visual stimuli in television, magazines, advertising, we have returned to a state of functional illiteracy akin to that of the medieval peasant, whose only knowledge came from the "reading" of stained-glass windows. Calligraphy, and the necessity to learn and copy model hands on the part of the student, helps to belie this doom-laden view — which may, in fact, not be true. It is good to have this latest addition to the literature of *optimism*, to craft and to knowledge.

WILLIAM HOGARTH

C C Ca C C Com

D D D

4

18

gghyjkk

klmnopp

19

grsst t

st st st

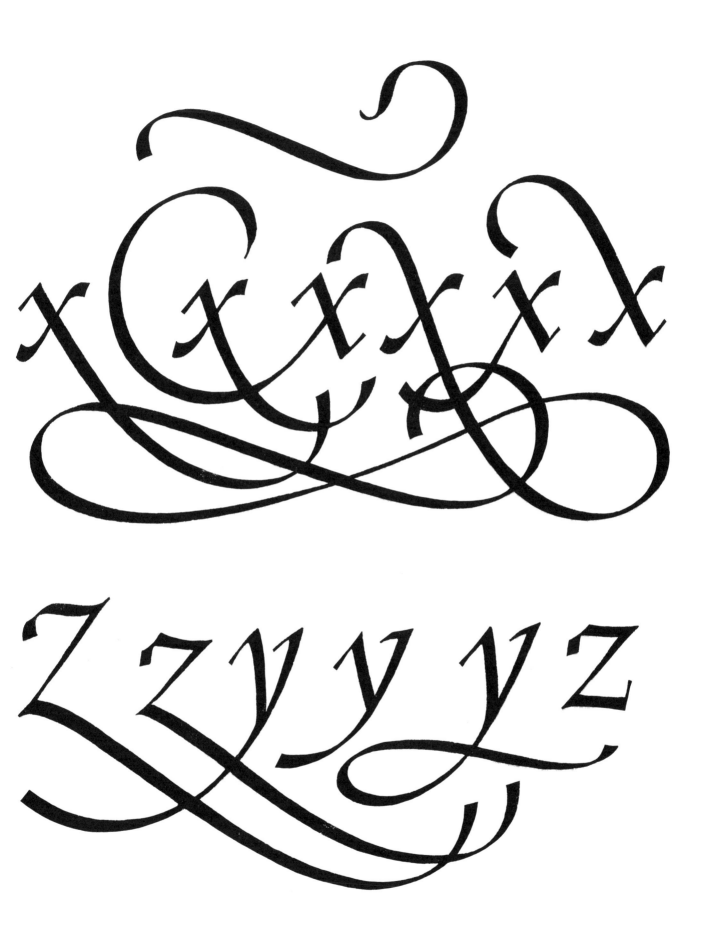